In Jesus' Name We Sing

Brief Choir Prayers

Fred H. Wilkins

CSS Publishing Company, Inc., Lima, Ohio

IN JESUS' NAME WE SING

For more information about CSS Publishing Company resources, visit our website at www.csspub.com.

ISBN 0-7880-1800-0 PRINTED IN U.S.A.

The devotions for church choirs which appear on the following pages are dedicated to the hundreds of singers who were musically influenced by Dr. Fred H. Wilkins for more than fifty years. These singers sang in the adult choirs of the churches in the State of California as follows:

Our Saviour's Lutheran Church, Long Beach

Ascension Lutheran Church, Rancho Palos Verdes

Christ the King Lutheran Church, Torrance

Community Presbyterian Church, South Gate

First Methodist Church, Gardena

First Lutheran Church, Inglewood

Saint Mark's Community Methodist Church, Los Angeles

Chapel, United States Naval Hospital, San Diego

Epworth Methodist Church, Los Angeles

Acknowledgments

Deep appreciation is acknowledged to Joan Cecille Anderson Wilkins, the author's wife, for her many years of devotion to him and support of his many projects related to church music. Personally, she has stamped and filed new anthems, mended thousands of old anthems, stuffed and stamped envelopes, prepared and served refreshments, entertained many choirs in her home, xeroxed letters and bulletins, and she has sung in his choir for over fifty years. All this while raising three children, teaching Sunday school for twenty years, serving as the financial secretary and the president of the congregation. These services to her Lord have been very much appreciated by many pastors and the singers of the various choirs in which she has sung — and especially by "Uncle Fred."

The author is deeply indebted to Adelyn Johnson of Long Beach, California, for her editing of the manuscript.

Dr. Fred H. Wilkins
Kihei, Maui, Hawaii

Preface

You give but little when you give of your possessions.

It is when you give of yourself that you truly give.

For what are your possessions but things you keep and guard for fear you may need them tomorrow?

There are those who have little and give it all.

These are the believers in life and the bounty of life, and their coffer is never empty.

There are those who give with joy, and that joy is their reward.

Through the hands of such as these God speaks, and from behind their eyes He smiles upon the earth.[1]

Table Of Contents

I — Opening Of The Choir Season
1. Choir Dedication Sunday 9
2. New Choir Season 9

II — Liturgical Seasons Of The Church Year
3. Advent/Christmas 9
4. Christmas Joy 10
5. Lent/Good Friday 10

III — Special Seasons Of The Church Year
6. Special Choral Music Service (Concert) 11
7. Thanks For Life 11
8. Thanks For Voice 12
9. Thanks For Talent 12
10. Thanks For Spiritual Food 13
11. Thanksgiving For Nature 13
12. Thanks For Material Support 14

IV — General Themes
13. Absent Singers 14
14. Acceptance 14
15. Choir Thanks 15
16. Church Staff 15
17. Commitment 16
18. Concerns 16
19. Diction 17
20. Excellence 17
21. Faith And Trust 17
22. Fresh And New 18
23. Growth 18
24. Humility 18
25. I Am God 19
26. Inspiration 19

27. Jesus, Our Shepherd 20
28. Joy And Radiance 20
29. Let Go 20
30. Lord, We Are Able 21
31. Love — Jesus In The Flesh 21
32. Love 22
33. Nature 22
34. No Condemnation 23
35. Our Birthright 23
36. Pastor/Minister 23
37. Peace 24
38. Praise 24
39. Reach Out 25
40. Release 25
41. Servant 26
42. Stewardship 26
43. Talent And Acceptance 27
44. Talent Combined 27
45. Unchurched 28
46. Unconditional Regard 28
47. Unique And Special 29
48. A Vessel 29
49. The Way 30
50. Worshiper 30
51. Worth 30
52. Worthy 31

V — End Of The Choir Season
53. Choir Recognition 31

Endnotes 32

Date Used: __________
By: ________________

1 — Choir Dedication Sunday

Here we are, O God, back again in the chancel to sing your praises for another season. Bless our diction that your Word may be heard and accepted by all those who have come to worship. In Jesus' Name, we pray. Amen.

Date used: __________
By: ________________

2 — New Choir Season

Dear Heavenly Father, we thank you for the privilege of coming together to sing your praises for one more season. Help us to show our love for you by our reverence.

Give us wisdom so that we might [illegible] commit ourselves to be faithful to you [illegible] of the seasons to come. In Jesus' Nam[illegible]

3 — Advent/Christmas

O Dear God, help us to look into our own hearts to see if we are truly ready to receive the Christ Child. Help us to examine our dedication to you by measuring the way we lead our lives against the example that Jesus taught us.

Help us to be honest, to share, and to find commitment in you. Help us to realize that we cannot serve you well with our strength alone. Give us courage, power, and direction.

May all that we commit of ourselves to you be richly blessed. We trust you to lead and inspire this choir to serve you well this Christmas season and always. In Jesus' Name we pray. Amen.

Date used: ___________
By: ________________

4 — Christmas Joy

JOY to the world! The Lord has come! O Dear God, may those who have come to worship this morning see the JOY in our faces and eyes. May they hear JOY in the songs that we sing. And may they sense the JOY that Jesus has come to dwell in our hearts. In his Name we sing. Amen.

Date used: ___________
By: ________________

5 — Lent/Good Friday

Our Loving Heavenly Father, we are concerned about the un-churched in our community. As you lead them to this tabernacle of love, help us to greet them with open arms and hearts filled with your love. May we see Jesus in their souls and connect the Jesus within our souls by accepting them totally, without judgment or criticism.

Just as on that first Good Friday you forgave each one of us for all of our past, present, and future mistakes, help us now and for the rest of our lives to be witnesses to the fact that Jesus and his love permeates our total beings: mind, soul, and spirit. In Jesus' Name we pray. Amen.

Date used: __________
By: ______________

6 — Special Choral Music Service

Dear God, you know how hard each member of this choir has worked to prepare for this special service of music. Now that all of the right notes are in place, the melodic lines are practically memorized, and we feel the rhythms in our very toes, help us to focus on the text — the message that tells in this grand and glorious manner the story of your love and of your dear Son, Jesus, the Christ.

Bless each singer and instrumentalist to be worthy to fill this holy tabernacle with this inspiring music, all to your honor, glory, and praise. In Jesus' Name we sing. Amen.

Date used: __________
By: ______________

7 — Thanks For Life

Almighty Heavenly Father, your name is holy, and we worship you. You have created us, and we seek to be worthy of your trust in us.

We thank you for this day;

- for the peace of mind that you have given to us,
- for the beautiful people whose lives we have touched,
- for our food and shelter and all other necessities of life,
- but mostly, we thank you for your everlasting arms which support us and bring meaning to this experience we call life.

Now as we enter your service of worship, remind us of your love for us. Let us be thankful for the talented composers and arrangers through whom you speak to your people, and take our talents and use them to your honor and glory this day and for all eternity. We pray in Jesus' Name. Amen.

Date used: 1/16/02
By: Adult Choir

8 — Thanks For Voice

O Dear God, we thank you for all of the gifts which you have given:

- for your love,
- for sending Jesus to show us how to live,
- for our country and the freedom we experience here,
- for this congregation, and
- for our pastor(s).

We especially thank you for our voices and the opportunity we have to sing your praises. Help us to use all of your gifts well so that this congregation will be enriched.

Accept our love for you; we want to serve you well all the days of our lives. ~~Help us to find the strength to commit ourselves again this morning to this end.~~ In Jesus' Name we pray. Amen.

Date used: 10/10/01
By: Adult Choir

9 — Thanks For Talent

Our Loving Heavenly Father, help us to be aware of the many gifts and talents which you have given to each one of us. Although we do not understand why we have been so richly blessed in these special ways, help us to accept these talents with joy.

As we realize that these skills come from you, may we see their high value and special worth and give you our thanks. Help us to see the beautiful qualities of others as gifts from you, too. Bless our service this ~~morning~~. Help us to sing well. In Jesus' Name we sing. Amen. evening.

Date used: ___________
By: ________________

10 — Thanks For Spiritual Food

Dear God, just as you care for the birds of the fields, you take care of each one of us. For this we greatly thank you. Feed us now in this service of worship with spiritual food.

Be with our pastor as he brings your Word. Open our ears, minds, and hearts to really hear your message of love. Bless us now as we sing, and direct us in this coming week to give your will a priority in our lives. In Jesus' Name we sing. Amen.

Date used: ___________
By: ________________

11 — Thanksgiving For Nature

Dear God, we thank you for the brightness and warmth of the sun, for the rain which brings forth our beautiful flowers and trees, and even for the wind and snow. These are all signs of your love for us and of your very presence here in your world.

Eternally, we give you thanks. Bless us now as we enter your sanctuary to sing your praise. Help us to sing well, for we give you the glory. In Jesus' Name we sing. Amen.

Date used: ___________
By: _______________

12 — Thanks For Material Support

Our Loving Heavenly Father, we pause for a brief moment this morning to say, "Thanks," for the equipment which supports this choir: our library of choral music, our pianos, organ, music stands, robes, and hymnals — all of the physical necessities it takes to make our ministry of music a success.

We thank you for the members of this congregation who tithe from the resources which you have given them to add this beauty to our worship. We sing our appreciation each Lord's day. In Jesus' Name we sing. Amen.

Date used: ___________
By: _______________

13 — Absent Singers

O Dear God, we lift up the names of our choir members who are not with us this morning. If they are ill, bring them health; if they are traveling, protect them and bring them safely home.

As we sing this morning, recreate us to be a blessing for you and your service. In Jesus' Name we sing. Amen.

Date used: ___________
By: _______________

14 — Acceptance

Dear Lord, help us to follow the model you demonstrated by your acceptance of our strengths and weaknesses.

As we accept and serve others in this community, may we know that we are accepting and receiving you. Bless us as we sing this morning, and keep us safe forever. In Jesus' Name we sing. Amen.

Date used: ___________
By: ________________

15 — Choir Thanks

O God, you are the source, the supply, and the bearer of all good gifts.

You have given yourself to us, and we are overwhelmed by your love. We appreciate this gift and continually seek to be worthy.

We lean upon you for strength, courage, and fortitude, and you are always there. We thank you for these singers — this choir. You have richly blessed this congregation and us.

Bless us now as we sing this morning. In Jesus' Name we sing. Amen.

Date used: ___________
By: ________________

16 — Church Staff

Our Loving Heavenly Father, we give you thanks this morning for our wonderful church staff:

- for our pastor who brings the Word each Sunday,
- for our director of music who selects the choral music which we sing and trains us to sing it well,
- for our organist who sets the mood for worship with preludes and offertories and accompanies our anthems,
- for our church secretary who supports us in so many ways, and
- for our custodian who cleans our rehearsal room so that we have a pleasant place to practice.

May all that these devoted servants do to make you and your Son, Jesus, come to life in worship, be supported well by each member of this choir. We sing to your honor and glory. In Jesus' Name we sing. Amen.

Date used: 10-3-01
By: Adult Choir

17 — Commitment

Dear God, as a family of choral singers, we begin this new season right where we are, with whom we are, and with what we have to offer. With your blessing, we know that we will sing with the angels, rejoicing and being glad in your love and service, realizing that we are making a tremendous contribution toward leading this congregation on a closer walk with you.

We feel our talents unfolding: help us to be conscious of our freedom to expand, making positive choices for you. We begin our service with whatever level of talent we have been endowed, knowing that you will take even our most meager attempts, bless them, and help them to grow.

We give you thanks for the honor, the blessing, and the privilege of serving you. In Jesus' Name, hear our prayer. Amen.

Date used: ____________
By: ________________

18 — Concerns

Dear God, be with us this morning as we sing our anthem. May our music be worthy of you. We especially bring to you the members of this congregation who are ill, lonely, depressed, and searching for their way. Use us as your instruments of love, caring, and compassion.

May we give a listening ear where needed or a helping hand to reach out as Jesus taught us to do. In his Name we sing. Amen.

Date used: ___________
By: ________________

19 — Diction

Dear God, we have a story to tell our congregation this morning. We have worked hard on our diction. May we now just forget all of the mechanics of language and focus on the message that our morning anthem can bring to the worshipers.

Bless us this morning, as you do each Lord's day, to sing well, for we give you all of the glory. In Jesus' Name we sing. Amen.

Date used: ___________
By: ________________

20 — Excellence

Dear God, we want to give you our best this morning as we sing your praises. Help us to produce the best tone, the best blend of song, and the finest diction possible to praise your Holy Name. In Jesus' Name we sing. Amen.

Date used: ___________
By: ________________

21 — Faith And Trust

Surely, our cause is with you, O Lord. In the shadow of your hand, protect us from all mistakes. We are your servants.

We want to bring only glory to your name. You are our strength. You have chosen us to serve you. Help us now to be faithful.

We call on the Name of our Lord Jesus to guide and direct us through this service. We put our trust and faith in you. Especially bless our singing together in one grand and glorious song of praise. We ask these things in the Name of Jesus, our Lord. Amen.

Date used: ___________
By: _________________

22 — Fresh And New

Dear God, help us not to get lost in the routine of our worship experience. May it never get so automatic or mundane that we recite and sing totally detached, without engaging our hearts, minds, and souls.

May the Lord's Prayer, the creeds, the liturgy, and the familiar hymns be fresh and new this morning — as though this were our first experience with them. Bless us as we sing to your honor and glory. In Jesus' Name we pray. Amen.

Date used: ___________
By: _________________

23 — Growth

Dear God, bless our service this morning. We look to the "right now" of our experience, and we know that, in the future, you will surely increase our number of singers so that we may serve you even better.

We trust you to balance our vocal parts so that we may sound really good. We seek to be a blessing to our congregation.

We bow in all humility. We are open to your guidance. In Jesus' holy Name we pray. Amen.

Date used: ___________
By: _________________

24 — Humility

The Lord is in his Holy Temple. Let all the earth keep silence before him.

Bless our singing, O Lord, that the sounds that we make may be beautiful and worthy of praising your holy Name. In Jesus' Name we pray. Amen.

Date used: ___________
By: ________________

25 — I Am God

Dear God, this congregation has worked very hard to build this beautiful sanctuary. Our stained glass windows tell the story of Jesus. As worshipers come in, they are moved by our majestic organ music.

Even the flowers and the paraments on the altar all speak the same message: "Be still and know that I am God."

As a choir, may we add to the beauty of this place and underscore the preaching of the Word by our magnificent pastor. In Jesus' Name we pray. Amen.

Date used: ___________
By: ________________

26 — Inspiration

Dear God, we especially thank you for the inner resources that give us the power to try and to keep on trying even when we are the most fearful of failing you.

We thank you for the inspiration of David, of Daniel, and of Paul from out of the distant past. Help us to follow Jesus when our way appears unclear.

Inspire us, lead us, and make us new creatures in Jesus. Bless our music this morning. May the worshipers be inspired. We pray in the Name of Jesus, our Lord. Amen.

Date used: ___________
By: ________________

27 — Jesus, The Shepherd

O Jesus, our faithful Shepherd, lead us in this service of worship to send a message through our songs of praise that you love everyone present in this house of prayer. We are the sheep of your pasture ready to follow whenever you may lead us. In Jesus' Name we sing. Amen.

Date used: ___________
By: ________________

28 — Joy And Radiance

Dear God, as we sing for you this morning, fill our hearts with joy and put a glow of radiance on our faces.

We sing our songs about Jesus, and we give you all of the praise, honor, and glory. In Jesus' Name we pray. Amen.

Date used: ___________
By: ________________

29 — Let Go

Our Loving Heavenly Father, we have prepared well our anthem and service music for this morning's service. We are ready to sing your praises during the next hour of worship.

Help us now to relax our physical bodies, to release and let go of all tension in our minds, and to focus only on your service of praise.

May all those who attend this morning be open to the pastor's preaching of the Word. Bless us as we sing. In Jesus' Name we pray. Amen.

Date used: ___________
By: ________________

30 — Lord, We Are Able

Our Heavenly Father, Jesus asked us if we were able to follow him. By our very presence here this morning, we are declaring our commitment to love and serve you. Lord, we are able — we are loyal in following his footsteps. Bless us now as we sing your praises. In Jesus' Name we pray. Amen.

Date used: ___________
By: ________________

31 — Love — Jesus In The Flesh

Dear God, in the scripture we are reminded that you are love. Jesus became love in the flesh and taught us in many ways that you love us, now and forevermore.

May everything that happens in this service of worship this morning emphasize that *love* message. Especially bless our music.

May our anthem come alive so that as each worshiper leaves this holy tabernacle, each one will know that he or she is loved, right down to the very marrow of their bones — in their very souls. In Jesus' Name we pray. Amen.

Date used: ___________
By: ________________

32 — Love

Dear God, as we read about love in Solomon's "Song of Songs," we are reminded of the love that you have for your people and of Christ's love for his church.

It is time now to sing, and we want you to hear the sound of our melodious voices. And as we sing our anthem this morning, we are reminded that love is more powerful than death, stronger than the grave. Love cannot be bought.[2]

You first loved us; from grateful hearts we love you. In Jesus' Name we pray. Amen.

Date used: ___________
By: ________________

33 — Nature

Dear God, we thank you for the setting sun over the ocean and mountains. We thank you, too, for the sunrise which reminds us that we have one more day to praise your Holy Name and to do your work among our fellow men, women, and children.

As we sing for you this morning, the beauty of our song comes from grateful hearts, overflowing with our love, dedication, and commitment to you, O Holy Father. We pray now in Jesus' Name. Amen.

Date used: __________
By: ______________

34 — No Condemnation

Dear God, we remember the story of Jesus and the woman who was about to be stoned. Just as he said, "Neither do I condemn you," help us to follow his example by giving up our critical and judgmental natures. Rather, may we see Jesus in the face of every man, woman, and child with whom we come in contact.

Help us to sing with beauty, joy, and thanksgiving this morning. In Jesus' Name we pray. Amen.

Date used: __________
By: ______________

35 — Our Birthright

O Lord, we know that you are God! You created us in your own spiritual image; therefore, we belong to you.[3] Help us now as we sing to bring Jesus and his teachings to this congregation. In his Name we sing. Amen.

Date used: __________
By: ______________

36 — Pastor/Minister

Dear God, we especially ask you to be with our pastor this morning as he brings the Word. May we support him in this service of worship with beautiful melodies, rich harmonies, and interesting rhythms — all to reach the hearts, minds, and souls of every worshiper. In Jesus' Name we sing. Amen.

Date used: ___________
By: _________________

37 — Peace

Our Loving Heavenly Father, we come before you in all humility. As we prepare for worship, clear our minds of all worry, concern, and trouble; help us to set aside the responsibilities of daily living and focus for this one sacred hour only on you and your Beloved Son, Jesus.

We ask for a sense of calm and tranquility to permeate every part of our being, but especially we request that perfect peace which Jesus promised us. Bless our singing this morning, for we ask it in Jesus' Name. Amen.

Date used: ___________
By: _________________

38 — Praise

Shout praises to the Lord, everyone on this earth. Be joyful and sing as you come in to worship the Lord![4] Sing to the Lord, all the world! Worship the Lord with joy; come before him with happy songs! Dear God, we do sing praises to you. Everyone in this choir bows his head in deep humility. Yet we are joyful and we sing in worship to you, O Lord. In Jesus' Name we sing. Amen.

Date used: __________
By: ______________

39 — Reach Out

Dear God, we know that you will bless our singing for this service. But after it is over, help us to reach out for the visitors, those that don't have a church home. Help us to encourage those who have been ill and those who have lost a loved one recently.

May we especially reach out for former choir members and others who love to sing. In the Name of Jesus, may we be missionaries to bring to the fold those who have a musical gift to share. In Jesus' Name we pray. Amen.

Date used: __________
By: ______________

40 — Release

Dear God, we close our eyes; we begin to relax. We release now all of the tension from our bodies. We feel the tension flowing out through our fingers and toes, right out of our physical beings.

As we relax, O God, we rest our troubled spirits on you. We thank you for giving us the freedom and the intellect to choose what is right for us. We are especially thankful for your giving us the creativity and the opportunity to serve you in this choir. Help us to sing well so that those who have come to worship this morning may leave inspired, ready to serve you daily. In Jesus' Name we pray. Amen.

Date used: ___________
By: ________________

41 — Servant

We know that at times our talents seem like a burden to us, O Lord. Others have a high expectation of our abilities and achievements. May we not respond to their urging and applause but only to that inner, small voice of joy and pleasure which says, "You have done a good job, thou good and faithful servant."

Bless our service this morning and give us the courage to continue to serve you all the days of our lives. In Jesus' Name we pray. Amen.

Date used: 10/17/01
By: Adult Choir

42 — Stewardship

Our Loving Heavenly Father, you have given us fine voices with which to make melody. Help us to use all of our talents well for your honor and glory. As we sing "all the day long," may it be with joy in our hearts.

Help us to be good stewards of our voices, to protect them from strain and harm. Be with us as we sing our ~~anthem this morning~~. In Jesus' Name we sing. Amen. this evening.

Date used: ___________
By: _______________

43 — Talent And Acceptance

Dear God, accept the talent of each one participating in this choir this morning. Some of us sing extremely well, and we have had considerable musical training. Others of us feel our musical contribution to be somewhat limited — or even unworthy of your service.

Help us not to make personal judgments of one another, but may we unite our voices in a common proclamation of our love for you.

Bless our music this morning. May its joy touch every heart that comes to worship. In Jesus' Name we sing. Amen.

Date used: ___________
By: _______________

44 — Talent Combined

Help us, O God, to use our combined talents effectively. We trust you to bless our development in the art of choral music and our personal devotion so that we may continue to sing your praises.

Protect us as we leave this sacred place and help us to return each Sunday, renewed, refreshed — ready to inspire — ready to share the joy of being your children. In Jesus' Name we sing. Amen.

Date used: ___________
By: ________________

45 — Unchurched

Dear God, we pray especially this morning for the visitors and any others in attendance who may not have a church home. Open their ears to hear the pastor's sermon; open their hearts to receive you as Lord.

May the music that we sing — anthems, hymns, liturgy, and spiritual songs — set the emotional tone to assist each one in this worship service to receive Jesus as Lord. In his holy Name we pray. Amen.

Date used: ___________
By: ________________

46 — Unconditional Regard

Dear God, help us to accept others just as you created them to be, without criticism or judgment of any kind. Help us to look for the beauty of Jesus in every person with whom we come in contact.

Please sing through us this morning as we come with minds and hearts cleared of anything negative or unlovely.

We are open now only to your love. In Jesus' Name we pray. Amen.

Date used: __________
By: ______________

47 — Unique And Special

O Dear God, we thank you for the individuality which makes this choir so unique and special in your sight. Help us to channel our personal individuality toward the unifying of one great and glorious sound, leading all worshipers to your Throne of Grace. Bless our singing this morning.

Thank you for your unending love. As we love you in return, may we also express our love toward one another. Bless us, for we ask these things in Jesus' Name. Amen.

Date used: __________
By: ______________

48 — A Vessel

Dear God:
You are the only power in the universe. You are God.
You are the only singer in the universe. You are God.

You are the chief musician.

- You write the music,
- You play the notes,
- You sing the songs, and
- You are God.

This choir sings and has its being in you, O Almighty God.

- Sing through us,
- Teach through us,
- Inspire through us, and
- Bless through us.

We give you our voices, our hearts, and our minds.
Take them, bless them, and use them, this day and forevermore —
Both in this world, and in the world to come.
In Jesus' Name we sing. Amen.

Date used: ___________
By: ________________

49 — The Way

Dear Jesus, you taught us that you are the Way. Help us this morning and all the days of our lives to follow in your footsteps. Through our pastor, speak to us in this service so that we may know how to follow your way, your truth, and your life.

May our music this morning support your message of love. We ask these things in your precious Name. Amen.

Date used: ___________
By: ________________

50 — Worshiper

Dear God, we pray for all those who have come to worship this morning. We know that you will provide loving support — food for their minds and hearts — verily, food for their souls.

May the music we present for this Sunday service serve to lighten burdens, to point in the direction of hope, and to put a smile on the face of every worshiper. We ask these things in Jesus' name. Amen.

Date used: ___________
By: ________________

51 — Worth

Our Loving Heavenly Father, it has been said that "our worth is not determined by the way that we feel about ourselves," but rather, "by how you feel about us."[5]

We know that you love us; we are yours. Sing through us this morning so that our anthem may bring inspiration to this service of worship and praise. In Jesus' Name we pray. Amen.

Date used: __________
By: ______________

52 — Worthy

Dear Lord Jesus, bless us as we attempt to serve you in beauty and holiness. Help us to remember that our Father made us worthy to call you our Brother. Remind us that our Father loves and accepts us in all of our humanness.

As we serve this congregation this morning, may we remember that we are serving you. Take our songs of praise and love and bless them. May they be vehicles for opening the hearts of men and women and boys and girls to your love. In Jesus' Name we pray. Amen.

Date used: __________
By: ______________

53 — Choir Recognition

Our Loving Heavenly Father, as we come to the last Sunday of our choir year, we know that we will be recognized , honored, praised, and valued by our beloved congregation.

It feels so good to be loved and to hear, "Thank you for a job well done." However, may we never forget that our singing has been dedicated unto you, O Lord.

You gave us the voices; you created talent in the composers, the choral conductors, and the organists. We simply want to say, "Thank you," for the privilege of singing your praises each Lord's day. We give you all the glory. In Jesus' Name we sing. Amen.

Endnotes

1. Gibran, Kahlil, *The Prophet.* Alfred A. Knopf, New York, N.Y., 1968.

2. Song of Songs (The Song of Solomon) 2:12, 14; 8:6-7.

3. Psalm 100:3.

4. Psalm 100:1-2.

5. From a sermon, "Beyond Looking Good," preached by Rev. Dennis P. Koch, Ascension Lutheran Church, Rancho Palos Verdes, California, on October 22, 1989.